THE MOST EXTREME CASE OF IDENTITY THEFT IN THE HISTORY OF THE WORLD

ISBN
978-1-5356-1684-3

WHO IS Y*SHUA

WHAT DOES YSHUA MEAN

WHAT DID HE DO
WHEN DID HE STOP
WHERE DID HE
PARTY
WHO DID HE HANG
WITH (EAT WITH)
WHY DID HE DIE

HOW DOES THIS
AFFECT ME

"Without Truth,
the human race is as
floating debris on an
ocean of madness"

YYMMinc@gmail.com

A SICK WORLD

Growing up, many of us were taught truth mixed with error. How many of you heard that if you did not accept Jesus as Lord and Saviour you would burn and be tortured in hell forever and ever, for all eternity? Does there seem to be much difference between having someone hold a knife to your throat and demand your allegiance to their religion or being threatened and kept in line with fear tactics? It seems that in the "Old Testament" Jehovah is mean and exacting, and in the "New Testament" Jesus is nice and liberal. He would never hurt anyone or demand a certain conduct or way of living. Is the Creator schizophrenic?! (Or are the gods schizophrenic?)

Here is how it is laid out in modern-day Christianity: I, man/Adam, disobeyed the Creator and was sentenced to live outside the Garden of Eden, eternally separated from him, until the seed of the woman would crush the snake's head and free me from the curse of the

LAW (TORaH), because time and time again I could not keep or obey it. So the Creator had to send his son to die for me, in my place, because only he could keep all of those laws. Then, after he died and rose from the dead, he changed the Law because it was just too difficult. So the question is WHY? Why did he not just change it to begin with and not have to see his son tortured, apparently for no reason? Certainly there must be a logical answer. I mean, if I made the Creator angry with my behaviour before, what makes it different now, except I said a little prayer and pay tithes?

CONTENTS

ONE

WHAT'S IN A NAME?

If Jesus were driving around in an automobile today, what kind of car would he drive?

Answer: A Christler

ONE NAME

ACTS 4.12
NEITHER IS THERE
SALVATION IN ANY
OTHER: FOR THERE IS
NONE OTHER NAME
UNDER HEAVEN
GIVEN AMONG MEN,
WHEREBY WE MUST
BE SAVED.

THIS SCRIPTURE IS EXCITING IN HE-
BREW, BUT NOT EASILY SEEN IN
ENGLISH. WE READ HEBREW FROM
RIGHT TO LEFT.

וְאֵין יְשַׁע בִּלְתּוֹ כִּי לֹא נִתַּן שֵׁם אַחֵר לִבְנֵי אָדָם תַּחַת הַשָּׁמַיִם אֲשֶׁר בּוֹ נִוָּשֵׁעָה

Look at the second and last words, *yeshai* and *nushaa'ah*: נושעה ישע these two words are formed from a two-letter (parent) root. ש ע *Eyeen* and *sheen* translate into English as "eye" and "tooth." The second word is translated as "salvation," and the last word as "saved." This is amazing in Hebrew, as it forms an integral part of the master's name! So if it is true that there is salvation (YSHUA) ישועה in only one name, then what is that name?

JESUS OR JOSHUA?

A SERMON BY PASTOR BROWN – A "SOUTHERN" BAPTIST PREACHER

Pastor Brown: Everybody, please turn in your Bibles to Acts, chapter seven, and starting with verse forty-four, read to verse forty-six. Okay, who wants to read? All right, Sister Susie, and read it loud and clear now.

Sister Susie: "Our ancestors had the tabernacle of the covenant law with them in the wilderness. It had been made as God directed Moses, according to the

12

pattern he had seen. After receiving the tabernacle, our ancestors under Joshua brought it with them when they took the land from the nations God drove out before them. It remained in the land until the time of David, who enjoyed God's favor and asked that he might provide a dwelling place for the God of Jacob."

Pastor Brown: Okay, thank you, Sister Susie. Now, who out there has a different version?

Brother Billy raises his hand.

Pastor Brown: Okay, Brother Billy, what does yours say?

Brother Billy: "Our fathers had the tabernacle of witness in the wilderness, as he had appointed, speaking unto Moses, that he should make it according to the fashion that he had seen. Which also our fathers that came after brought in with Jesus into the possession of the Gentiles, whom God drave out before the face of our fathers, unto the days of David; Who found favour before God, and desired to find a tabernacle for the God of Jacob."

Pastor Brown: Now, who all sees a difference between these two Bibles? Go ahead, Sister Agnes; tell us what you see.

Sister Agnes: Well, in Sister Susie's version it says Joshua, but in Brother Billy's it says Jesus. !Hey, whats going on here, Pastor?

Pastor Brown: Well, let me try to explain. Sister Susie, what Bible translation did you read from?

Sister Susie: NIV.

Pastor Brown: And Brother Billy, what was yours?

Brother Billy: King James.

Pastor Brown: Well, you see, every time the King James translators came across this name in the Greek they translated it into English as Jesus. Every time, now! However, these here newer Bibles – most, if not all, translate it as Jesus except in two places: one here, and the other in the book of Hebrews, chapter four, verse eight. You see, when you are translating from one language to another and you get to a name, you don't technically translate it; you transliterate it. Meaning you try to put letters together to form a word that sounds like the word you are translating.

Okay, now turn to Acts, chapter four, verse twelve. Who wants to read? Okay, Brother Jim Bob, go ahead.

Brother Jim Bob: "Neither is there salvation in any other: for there is none other name under heaven given among men, whereby we must be saved."

Pastor Brown: Thank you, Brother Jim Bob. So – there is one name by which we are to be saved; what is that name, everybody?

PART OF THE CONGREGATION SHOUTS JESUS AND THE OTHER JOSHUA.

Pastor Brown: I heard y'all say Jesus and Joshua; that's two names, now! Let's try again – what is our saviour's name, everybody?

THEY SHOUT LOUDER BOTH NAMES.

Pastor Brown: Hallelujah, y'all have a disagreement! That's good and should cause us to stretch and grow! Our goal for this week should be to research and get some light on this subject, as our salvation appears to depend upon it. Okay, Brother Ralph, would you close us in prayer?

HERE ENDS PASTOR BROWN'S SERMON

Suggested reading: Exodus 3

TWO

TURN NOT TO THE RIGHT OR THE LEFT

WHEN DID HE STOP

1 Moses 2.1-3   Also Known As Genesis 2:1-3
Thus the heavens and the earth were finished, and all the host of them. And on the seventh day Elohim [commonly rendered in English as God] ended his work which he had made; and he rested on the seventh day from all his work which he had made. And Elohim blessed the seventh day, and sanctified it: because that in it he had rested from all his work which Elohim created and made.

2 Moses 20.8-11   AKA Exodus 20:8-11
Remember the sabbath day, to keep it holy. Six days shalt thou labour, and do all thy work: But the seventh day is the sabbath of the LORD [יהוה, YHWH,

17

sometimes pronounced Yahweh or Yehovah] thy Elohim: in it thou shalt not do any work, thou, nor thy son, nor thy daughter, thy manservant, nor thy maidservant, nor thy cattle, nor thy stranger that is within thy gates: For in six days YHWH made heaven and earth, the sea, and all that in them is, and rested the seventh day: wherefore YHWH blessed the sabbath day, and hallowed it.

2 Moses 31.12+13

And YHWH spake unto Moses, saying, Speak thou also unto the children of Israel, saying, Verily my sabbaths ye shall keep: for it is a sign between me and you throughout your generations; that ye may know that I am YHWH that doth sanctify you.

5 Moses 5.32

Ye shall observe to do therefore as YHWH your Elohim hath commanded you: ye shall not turn aside to the right hand or to the left.

Joshua 23.6

Be ye therefore very courageous to

keep and to do all that is written in the book of the law of Moses, <u>that ye turn not aside therefrom to the right hand or to the left;</u>

Proverbs 4.27

<u>Turn not to the right hand nor to the left:</u> remove thy foot from evil.

Now, if we put the days of the week in a circle – which indeed they are – they could look like this.

Do you know on which day Yeshua (Jesus) rested?

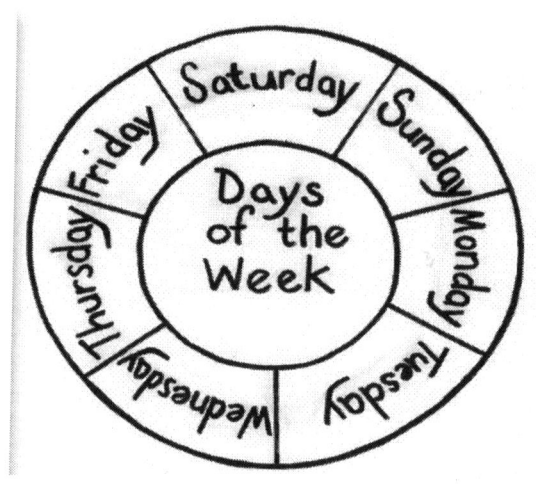

Do you know what days are considered holy for Christians and Muslims?

Suggested reading: Genesis 1

THREE

TIME TO PARTY (THE HOLY (special) DAYS OF YHWH)

WHERE SHALL WE MEET

3 Moses 23.1+2   Leviticus 23.1+2

And YHWH spake unto Moses, saying, speak unto the children of Israel, and say unto them, Concerning the feasts of YHWH, which ye shall proclaim to be holy convocations, <u>even these are my feasts</u>.

Notice that these feasts are not Jewish, but belong to YHWH. It is important to comprehend who we are. The following scriptures declare we are to be identified with Yshua the Hebrew/Israeli/Jew and his family. We are not second-class citizens. We are all ONE in Yshua. We are the children of Abraham. Who is

Israel? Those who follow Yahshua, the Son of Joseph, - - - the Son of Jacob, the Son of Isaac, the Son of Promise, the Seed of Abraham and Celebrate / guard / keep YHWH's commandments.

John 17.20+21   Yshua speaking

My prayer is not for them alone. I pray also for those who will believe in me through their message, that all of them may be <u>one</u>, Father, just as you are in me and I am in you. May they also be in us so that the world may believe that you have sent me.

Are the people of the Book ONE today? How many denominations are there in Christianity? How many sects in Judaism? So can we all, or most all, admit that we are fouled up?

My prayer is not for them alone. I pray also for those who will believe in me through their message, that all of them may be <u>one</u>, Father, just as you are in me and I am in you. May they also be in us so that the world may believe that you have sent me.

So let's ask the question again. Are we ONE? Are the so-called people of the Book one? Are Muslims and Christians one? Are Christians and Jews one? Are Jews one? Are Christians one? Are Muslims? Don't Muslims, Christians, and Jews claim that it began with Abraham and Moses?

ONE LAW

2 Moses 12.48+49

And when a stranger shall sojourn with thee, and will keep the passover to YHWH, let all his males be circumcised, and then let him come near and keep it; and he shall be as one that is born in the land: for no uncircumcised person shall eat thereof.

What do you think? The Creator of everything said you would be as one born in the land. What land? America? No. Israel. And what would you be called if you lived in Israel?

3 Moses 24.22

Ye shall have <u>one manner of law</u>, as well for the stranger, as for one of your own country: for I am YHWH your Elohim.

4 Moses 15.16

<u>One law and one manner</u> shall be for you, and for the stranger that sojourneth with you.

!HOW MANY LAWS?

How long will the TORaH/Law remain?

Matthew 5.18   Yshua speaking

For verily I say unto you, <u>Till heaven and earth pass,</u> one jot or one tittle shall in no wise pass from the law, till all be fulfilled.

It is quite clear that the heaven and earth have not passed away. It appears that a major problem we have here is that in most Bibles the Hebrew word TORaH is translated as law. However, Torah does NOT necessarily mean law; it means instruction and teaching! So when someone says we are not under the law, they may not realize that they are actually saying, "I have nothing to do with the teaching and instruction of YHWH." *OoUuCcHh!!* I wonder if that is why chaos and division seem to abound in modern-day Christianity?

Ezekiel 20.19+20

I am YHWH your Elohim; walk in my statutes, and keep my judgments, and do them; And hallow my <u>sabbaths</u>; and they shall be a sign between me and you, that ye may know that I am YHWH your Elohim.

"Sabbaths" is a synonym for feast days. It's a party and he/they (Elohim is masculine plural) give(s) us guidelines and instructions for how to party/feast. Except for the Day of Atonement, I have seen no place that says we are not to eat, drink, and be merry. He even seems to suggest something like vodka or whiskey! Check out Deuteronomy 14.26.

4 Moses 16.16

Three times a year all your men must appear before YHWH your Elohim <u>at the place he will choose</u>: at the Festival of <u>Unleavened Bread</u>, the Festival of

Weeks and the Festival of Tabernacles. No one should appear before YHWH empty-handed:

Passover begins Unleavened Bread   John 2.13
       When it was almost time for the Jewish Passover, Yshua went up to _Jerusalem_.

Haha. Notice "Jewish Passover" in the translation. :-)

Suggested reading: Leviticus 23

       Have you ever wondered why or how Jewish people just can't or don't seem to see that Jesus is the Messiah?

FOUR

MONKEY BRAINS (CREATURES NOT MEANT TO EAT)

PROFANE VS PURE

I believe this next scripture is the first record in history of deviled ham. :-)

Matthew 8.32
And he (Yshua) said unto them (the devils), Go. And when they were come out, they went into the herd of swine: and, behold, the whole herd of swine ran violently down a steep place into the sea, and perished in the waters.

3 Moses UIQRA ויקרא
11.1-8   Animals declared food by Elohim

And YHWH spake unto Moses and to Aaron, saying unto them, Speak unto the children of Israel, saying, These are the beasts which ye shall eat among all the beasts that are on the earth. Whatsoever parteth the hoof, and is clovenfooted, and cheweth the cud, among the beasts, that shall ye eat. Nevertheless these shall ye not eat of them that chew the cud, or of them that divide the hoof: as the camel, because he cheweth the cud, but divideth not the hoof; he is unclean unto you. And the coney, because he cheweth the cud, but divideth not the hoof; he is unclean unto you. And the <u>hare</u>, because he cheweth the cud, but divideth not the hoof; he is unclean unto you. <u>And the swine</u> (pig), though he divide the hoof, and be clovenfooted, yet he cheweth not the cud; <u>he is unclean to you. Of their flesh shall ye not eat, and their carcase shall ye not touch; they are unclean to you.</u>

Now, if you think you gotta have your bacon (pig) and eggs and hash browns, too, that's your prerogative. The Creator does have something else to say about it however, check out Isaiah 66.17. Give thanks to him, especially after your meal (Deuteronomy 8.10). You may find that turkey bacon is a great substitute. Turkey pepperoni for pizza! Yum yum. He loves us; we really don't have to give up anything except for our lives (Matthew 16.24). If you begin keeping/celebrating Shabbat/Sabbath you may feel like you have been robbed all the days you did not. What a blessing! Don't let anyone tell you, you're under a curse because you keep your special date! Our Father's word/commandments.

Romans 14.14   Paul
    I know, and am persuaded by the Lord Jesus, that there is nothing unclean of itself: but to him that esteemeth any thing to be unclean, to him it is unclean.

    What? Wow! Could this be why the world is all (or most all) fouled up today?! People doing what is right in their own eyes? Maybe the reason some Jewish people don't see that Yshua is the long-awaited messiah is that he is not recognizable. The Christian world has him dressed up like Santa Claus, the Easter Bunny, the Tooth Fairy, or___? He does not line up with what the scriptures say. He's got strips of juicy bacon (pork) hanging out the side of his mouth. He celebrates Easter, Halloween, and Christmas (Saturnalia) instead of Passover, Tabernacles, and Chanukah. IF he rests it's on Sunday, the first day of the week, and not on the seventh day, Sabbath/Saturday. Oddly, his name in South America (*HeySus*) translates back into Hebrew as The Horse. The Satan/Enemy has a counterfeit/substitute for practically everything the Creator has made or done. The name of our Creator, the day of the week he hallows/sets apart, his festivals/holydays, eating habits, ya-da-yada-yada.

Here is a word picture comparing and con-trasting the AntiChrist with the Christ:

*

LORD VS YHWH

JESUS VS YESHUA

SUNDAY VS SATURDAY

EASTER VS PASSOVER PSACH

HALLOWEEN VS TABERNACLES

CHRISTMAS VS CHANUKAH

COMMON VS CLEAN

PIG VS COW

--

SUMMARY

Synopsis;   Seeing Together

Abba, Please help me be a better being/person
    Matthew 5

Yshua
In a nutshell Yshua means Deliverance/Salvation.
If there is one name under heaven whereby we must be saved, it must be Yshua or Joshua or___? Because the name/word Jesus did not exist four hundred years ago.

The Seventh Day
The Sabbath is huge; however, we should not make a religion out of it. Shabbat connects with the other feast days.

JeruSalem
The people of YHWH (Israel) go up to Jerusalem three times a year for the feasts. Since the Temple has been destroyed, and Yshua's

words in John 4.21-24, I am not sure how it is suppose to work out.

In modern-day terms we might say he hung out with politicians and porn stars. While this may be true, it is important to remember the influence that he had on people.

Clean Animals

Today, thanks to the laboratory, we can understand some reasons why we are not supposed to eat certain animals. For example, the cholesterol in shrimp and the worms in pork.

Except for the blood of the lamb, it appears the gentiles have it totally wrong. It seems the main thing Yshua has done is win the Victory over death. I think we can most all agree that he is a good teacher. So, if that is the case, some of the most powerful things he has been reported as saying are to penetrate the heart/core, so as to be a better human.

This quote is from a first century historian, JOSEPHUS, Book 18, Chapter 3, Paragraph 3, Verse 63-64.

Now, there was about this time Jesus, a wise man, if it be lawful to call him a man, for he was a doer of wonderful works-a teacher of such men as receive the truth with pleasure. He drew over to him both many of the Jews, and many of the Gentiles. He was [the] Christ; and when Pilate, at the suggestion of the principal men amongst us, had condemned him to the cross, those that loved him at the first did not forsake him, <u>for he appeared to them alive again the third day</u>, as the divine prophets had foretold these and ten thousand other wonderful things concerning him; and the tribe of Christians, so named from him, are not extinct at this day.

Acts 4.12 Hebrew, taken from Salkinson-Ginsburg, The Rev. Dr. Eric S. Gabe (2000)

Made in the USA
Columbia, SC
14 November 2020